W9-CIM-865

HELPING CHILDREN WATCH TV

A practical handbook of TV-related learning activities designed to make television the ally of parents and teachers—instead of the enemy.

by Nicholas A. Roes
Illustrated by CARU

PUBLISHED BY TEACHER UPDATE, INC., BOX 205, SADDLE RIVER, NEW JERSEY 07458

IN MEMORY OF TOMMY EVANS

ISBN 0-89780-030-3

CONTENTS

INTRODUCTION 6

WHERE TO BEGIN............................ 8

CAN SUPERMAN REALLY FLY? 12

GAME SHOWS................................17

WITH THE SET ITSELF 20

THE TV NEWS................................24

HOW TO MAKE AND USE A PLAY TV 28

TV ENGLISH LESSONS......................32

AND NOW A WORD FROM OUR SPONSOR ..37

ESPECIALLY FOR PARENTS................40

FOOD FOR THOUGHT 44

EPILOGUE....................................48

INTRODUCTION

The statistics are frightening: BEFORE A CHILD REACHES THE FIRST GRADE, HE OR SHE HAS ALREADY VIEWED 4,000 HOURS OF TV. Often times teachers must spend precious classroom hours helping students "unlearn" what TV has taught them. Some children cannot separate what is real from what is not; others cannot distinguish between commercials and programming. Low levels of interest in reading have been blamed on the television set. BY THE TIME A CHILD IS FOURTEEN YEARS OLD, HE OR SHE WILL HAVE ALREADY WITNESSED 11,000 TELEVISED MURDERS. Television has been accused of brutalizing our children and encouraging apathy and indifference.

IT HAS BEEN ESTIMATED THAT CHILDREN SPEND THREE TIMES AS MUCH TIME WITH THE TELEVISION SET AS THEY DO WITH THEIR CLASSROOM TEACHER. Teachers, parents and educational institutions—often on shoestring budgets—cannot possibly compete with the multi-million dollar budgets of TV stations for the attention of their children.

What parents and teachers can do is to help make the time that children spend with the television more productive. This book offers suggestions for teachers and parents to help make TV a more positive force in their children's development. It is a practical handbook of activities that will help your children deal with television more effectively. Television should be used to promote creativity—not stifle it. The activities in this book can be adapted for use with almost any age child, and we hope they will help you make TV your ally instead of your enemy.

Where to Begin

START
HERE

WHERE TO BEGIN

Take a survey—In order to use television effectively, you must become familiar with your children's viewing habits. Parents should talk with their children, and teachers should use a written survey or a show of hands (depending on age group).

Try to obtain the following information: Number of hours of TV watched each day, favorite types of programs (westerns, news, comedies, variety shows, etc.), specific favorites, and educational and news shows watched. Teachers may wish to have members of the class take this survey as a group project.

Discuss the nature of TV—How should it be used? Should its main purpose be entertainment or education? Try to impress upon your children the fact that TV watching is a skill we should all try to develop fully, so we can get the most out of the time we spend with the television.

Plan ahead—Let your children know when an especially good program is on. Keep informed of all children's programming so that you can keep your children informed when shows suitable to your children's interest and ability are aired.

Take a field trip—A trip to a local TV station will give your children a better understanding of how TV really works. They will soon discover that television shows are put together by real people just like them, and that there is nothing magical or mystical about it.

Make a list—List with your children other leisure time activities which are alternatives to TV viewing. Try to think of as many as you can. Discuss the relative merits of listening to music, sports activities, playing cards, etc.

Use TV as a lead-in—Situations in your children's favorite programs can be used as springboards for parent-child or classroom discussions.

CAN Superman Really Fly?

CAN SUPERMAN REALLY FLY?

The activities in this chapter are designed to help your children distinguish TV fantasy from reality.

Arrange for your children to talk with a police officer about TV cop shows. Many officers will be happy to explain their daily routine, and how it differs from what TV policemen do. Your children will probably have many questions. Afterwards, discuss with your children other occupations which might not be exactly as they seem to be on TV.

Discuss the meaning of the word ''stereotype''. Give examples of ethnic and other stereotypes and how they are reinforced by some TV shows. Ask how these one dimensional characters differ from real people.

Ask your children to remember three things they see

on television which could never happen in real life. Have your children share their examples and tell why these things could never really happen.

Discuss the difference between real life and TV violence. Actors who are wounded badly in one scene are often completely recovered and performing heroics in the next scene. Actors and actresses who die on one program often reappear on another.

Ask your children a series of questions like these: Can a can of spinach really make someone strong enough to lift up a house? (no) Were there ever any actual fights between Indians and settlers in American history? (yes) Can Superman really fly? (no) Do people really get to keep the money and prizes won on game shows? (yes—except for taxes).

Have your children draw pictures of something that happens on TV but not in real life. Then ask them to draw pictures of something that happens in real life but not on television (such as a product not performing as in a commercial, or a foolish mistake made by a hero).

Game Shows

GAME SHOWS

Most children are familiar with game shows. Some of the formats used on popular game shows can be adapted for reviewing material your children have learned. Classroom versions of game shows can make reviewing otherwise tedious information fun.

In some game shows time is a very important element. Depending on the age and ability of your children, game show formats could be used to reinforce time telling skills, or more advanced concepts.

There are also game shows which could inspire children to develop motor coordination. Teachers and parents can invent obstacle courses or other motor activities children will enjoy doing.

An example of one activity you may wish to use: ''Name That Place'' is a game in which facts are given about a city, a state, a continent, or a province. If the right answer is guessed on the first clue, the maximum number of points are won. The number of points given for guessing correctly decreases with each additional clue given.

These game show tournaments are best used when individual improvement over past performances is stressed, rather than competition with other children.

With the Set Itself

WITH THE SET ITSELF

The following activities are among the many ways children can learn from the TV set itself.

Show your children the inside of a TV set. This is an excellent lead-in for a study of electricity. Your children will have many questions during discussion of the many uses of electricity. Experiments with batteries are also popular with young children. Also include the story of how electricity was discovered.

Television can also be used in lessons on sound. Explain how it travels, how we can hear, and what makes sound. With older children you may want to include information on parts of the ear, or experiments with speakers. Younger children enjoy listening to the different sounds that are made when glasses filled with different amounts of water are struck.

Younger children can also learn math from the television dial or a facsimile. Ask them such questions as "How many channels between 2 and 7?" and "If I start at 11 and turn the dial backwards four channels, what channel will I be on?" These games reinforce basic counting skills, as well as help children learn beginning addition and subtraction.

TV NEWS

NOW FOR THE NEWS...

THE TV NEWS

Have your children monitor different news programs to compare lead stories, and the ratio of local to national news. Ask them to compare the treatment of the same stories on different channels. Have them draw conclusions and rate each news show in their survey.

Ask your children to compare television to newspapers. Make lists of the advantages and disadvantages of each method of reporting news. Ask your children which they prefer and why.

Communication skills can be developed by encouraging children to interview people they know. These interviewees could be parents, teachers, friends, relatives, or the principal. Have children make oral or written reports on what they have learned from their interviews.

Children may enjoy collecting information of interest

to local youngsters and then ''broadcasting'' interesting items at home or in school.

Older students might enjoy panel discussions on topics which are currently in the news. These round table talks could also be devoted to issues which concern students, such as school dress codes and other regulations.

How to Make and Use a Play TV

HOW TO MAKE AND USE A PLAY TV

To make a play TV for your playroom or classroom, you will need a box large enough for a child to stand in. Large appliance boxes from refrigerators or washers are best. Cut a "screen" in the top half of the box, so your children's top halves will be visible when they stand behind the box. Paint some knobs and dials on the box and you're ready to go.

In your play TV children can "recap" the days events, just as news shows do. This helps develop communication skills and is also an excellent source of feedback for parents and teachers. Children will report what they liked and disliked about each day.

Have your children write commercials for their favorite foods. Then ask them to appear on your play

TV and tell why they like this food and why others should buy some.

Children can report events of interest which happen in and around home and school on their play television. Ask your children if they feel any different now that they are TV stars.

A play TV can also be made from a smaller box, about the same size as a real TV. Cut an 8¼ by 11 inch "screen" on which children's sketches and paintings can be viewed. If possible, obtain a long roll of paper and have children draw illustrations on it. Insert two broomstick handles, parallel to the floor, through the box. These broomsticks should not be visible on the screen. Wrap the rolled up pictures on the bottom handle and tape the top part to the top handle. Children can now narrate a story as they show their pictures on the play TV by rolling the handles.

TV English Lessons

ABCDE
TV

TV ENGLISH LESSONS

Today's children can learn by giving TV show reports many of the same things we learned giving book reports. Children can relate the plot, comment on the development of characters, and give a general critique of any TV show. These TV show reports can be oral or written, and they usually inspire more enthusiasm in students than book report assignments.

Younger children can make lists of TV titles with proper nouns, or double consonants, or past tense verbs, or long vowel sounds, or adjectives, etc. In this way children learn alphabet sounds and parts of speech by reviewing the titles of their favorite shows.

Ask your children to listen for new words or phrases while they are watching television. These new words and phrases can be brought into class and shared, or they can be talked over with parents. Be certain that the meanings of these new words and phrases is clear.

TV shows often encourage children to read, despite what the critics of television say. Many of today's shows are based on books, and children should be encouraged to read these. News items and biographies of TV stars are also read by children with much enthusiasm. Books have also been inspired by successful TV shows, and often these books survive long after the TV series has been cancelled.

Children will probably enjoy comparing the books they have read to the TV movie versions. The advantages and disadvantages of each art form could be discussed, both in general and with specific shows.

Make a list with your children of TV related vocabulary words. Have them use these in conversation as often as possible. You may wish to add a few difficult words to the list to challenge the most advanced children.

Assign your students (or ask your child) to view a specific show at a specific time. Later, discuss the plot and message (if any). Also get your children's opinions on repeating this activity. Perhaps they would like to view and discuss a different type of show next time.

Older students could be encouraged to write a screenplay for their favorite TV show. This could be done individually or as a group project. It might even be fun to submit the script to the station which airs that particular show.

Younger students could role play their favorite TV characters and improvise a plot. Or, children could act out the action to a TV script as you narrate.

AND NOW A WORD FROM OUR SPONSOR

AND NOW A WORD FROM OUR SPONSOR...

The activities below are designed to help your children deal with TV commercials.

Do a taste test in class or at home and get a response from all the participants. Recommendations could be made of the basis of taste test results.

Have your children do a "consumer report" on a TV-advertised product to see if it lives up to its advertising claims. This report could include cost compared to similar products, special features, and life of the product.

Let your children prepare a "Junk Food Report". Compare nutrition information on the packages of different snacks and sweets to determine which are most harmful and which are least harmful.

Discuss the use of an attractive man or an attractive woman in commercials to encourage members of the opposite sex to buy a product. Does this approach work?

Older children may wish to monitor TV ads and prepare a report on the different types of television commercials. They could be divided into product categories and then subdivided according to the approach used by the advertiser.

Have your children make a 60 second TV commercial for their favorite school subject. It should include the most important information about this subject, explaining why it is needed.

Especially for Parents

ESPECIALLY FOR PARENTS

Teachers should encourage parents to use some of the following suggestions:

Children, as well as adults, should make up their minds ahead of time what to watch on television instead of just flipping on the set automatically to see what is on.

Try not to use the TV as a babysitter. Instead try to learn with your child as you watch television together. Make sure to discuss and explain what you have watched with your child if he or she wants to.

Read to your child. This encourages him or her to use imagination to create mental pictures. Pictures in the mind are often far more interesting and exciting than those on the TV screen.

Substitute parent-child activities for at least one hour of your TV viewing time each week. The TV won't miss you and you will get to know your child better.

Both mothers and fathers should be actively involved in their children's education. Take an active interest in what your child is doing at home and in school.

Food for Thought

IDEA
IDEAS

FOOD FOR THOUGHT

The following activities are best suited for older children, but they may be adapted for use with younger children and a different level of discussion.

Discuss the social value of television and the ways in which TV might be put to better use in the future.

Aggression and violence have also been related to television viewing. Does television help us deal with our violent tendencies or make it harder to control them? Are there instances where a certain amount of TV violence is necessary for the integrity of the plot?

The fact that television helps provide role models for children and sometimes reinforces stereotypes could also be a topic of discussion. Do children try to imitate the actions of TV characters? What should be done about shows which glorify the bad guys?

Discuss government censorship. Should our government be allowed to control TV more than it does now, to be sure that it serves the needs of the people? Should sex and violence go unchecked on television? Should TV shows be permitted to reinforce ethnic stereotypes? Should advertisers be allowed to make unfounded claims?

Epilogue

EPILOGUE

Many parents and teachers feel inadequate competing with television. This book will hopefully give them the means to deal with TV more effectively. But we should not lose sight of larger long range goals. The learning activities that are suggested in this book help us deal with TV in the here and now, but they are only an interim measure.

We must all—parents, teachers, networks, and sponsors—work together on several fronts, so that television can achieve its fullest potential. Our ultimate goal is to make TV a vehicle for providing us with maximum comfort and happiness, and to use it to promote the general welfare by keeping us entertained and well informed, and by challenging our imagination.

NOTES: